I0484787

Production Management

:: Author ::

Hetal Parmar

(M.COM., M.Phil., SLET)

PUBLISHED BY

The New Era International Publishing House
HQ. At & Po. Chaveli., Ta- Chansma,
Dist- Patan, North Gujarat, India, Asia.
www.iphouseindia.com

Production Management

First Publication: 16th FEBRUARY, 2015

Copyright: Author

(c) Hetal Parmar

ISBN:- 978-15-08712-29-9

Price: Rs.750/- INDIA

$ 15 OUTSIDE INDIA

PUBLISHED BY

The New Era International Publishing House
HQ. At & Po. Chaveli., Ta- Chansma,
Dist- Patan, North Gujarat, India, Asia.
www.iphouseindia.com

Content

LESSON : 1

ROLE AND SCOPE OF PRODUCTION MANAGEMENT, CONCEPT OF PRODUCTION MANAGEMENT

MEANING OF PRODUCTION

Production is an intentional act of producing something in an organized manner. It is the fabrication of a physical object through he use of men, material and some function which has some utility e.g. repair of an automobile, legal advice to a client, banks, hotels, transport companies etc.

Thus irrespective of the nature of organization, production is some act of transformation, i.e. inputs are processed and transformed into some output. The main inputs are information, management, material, land, labour and capaital. Fig. shown below explains the production process of an organization.

PRODUCTION PROCESS SYSTEM

INPUT   PROCESS   OUTPUT

_____

1

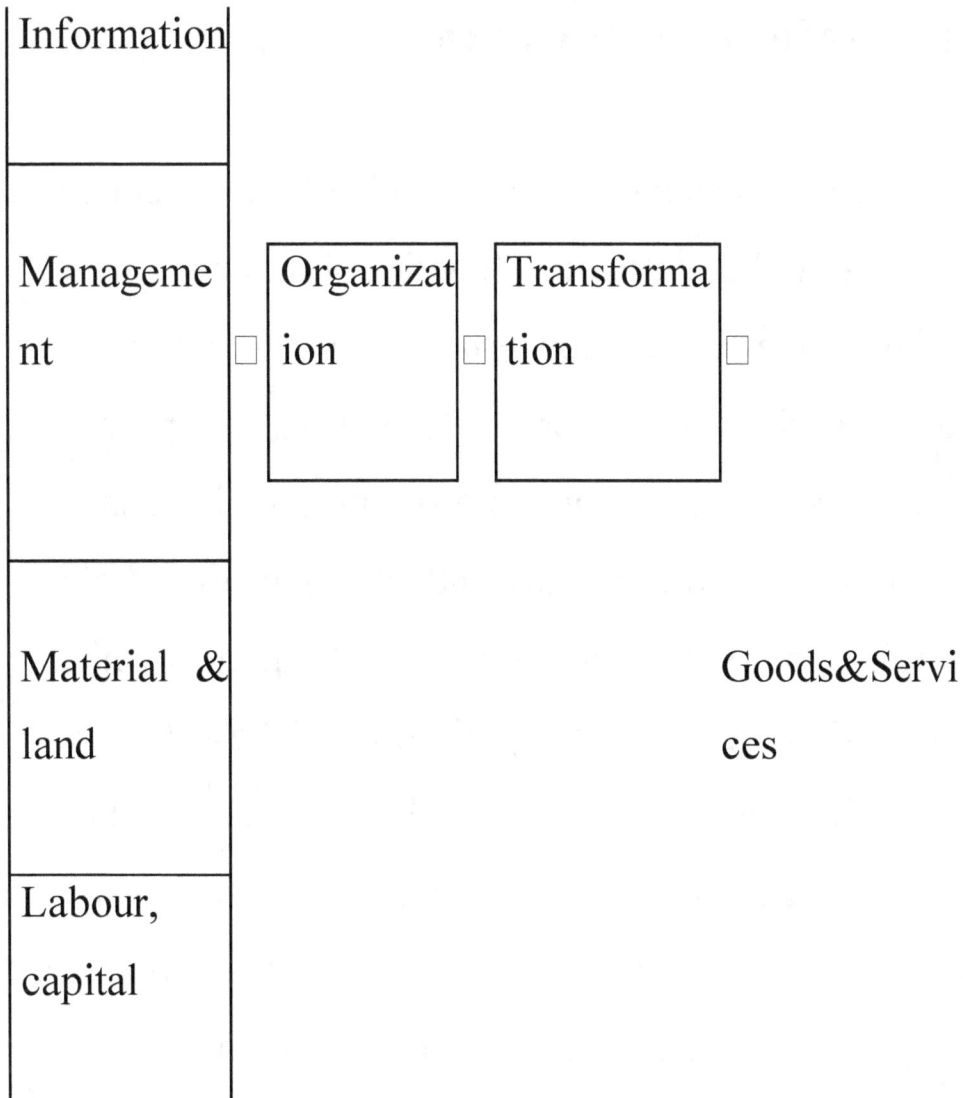

Labour, capital Thus the basis of Production is the transformation of inputs into goods and services. The main objectives of a production process are :

(i) optimum use of resources at optimum cost.

(ii) manufacture of the desired quality and quantity of goods and services.

Meaning of Production Management

Production management is a branch of management which is related to the production function. Production may be referred to as the process concerned with the conversion inputs (raw materials, machinery, information, manpower, and other factors of production) into output (semi finished and finished goods and services) with the help of certain processes (planning, scheduling and controlling etc.) while management is the process of exploitation of these factors of production in order to achieve the desired results. Thus production management is the management which by scientific planning and regulation sets into motion the part of an enterprise to which it has been entrusted the task of actual transformation of inputs into output. A few definitions of production management are being reproduced hereunder to understand the meaning of the term clearly :

(i) "Production management then becomes the process of effectively planning and regulating the operations of that part of an enterprise which is responsible for actual transformation of materials into finished products".

The definition seems to be quite incomplete as it ignores the human factors involved in a production process and lays stress only on the materialistic features.

Elwood S. Buffa has defined the term in a broader sense as :

(ii) "Production management deals with decision making related to production process so that the resulting goods or services are produced according to specifications in amounts and by the schedules demanded, and at a minimum cost".

Thus production management is concerned with the decision making regarding the production of goods and services at a minimum cost according to the demands of the customers through the management process of planning, organizing and controlling. In order to attain these objectives, effective planning and control of production activities is very essential. Otherwise, the customers shall remain unsatisfied and ultimately certain-activities may have to be closed.

Production management, thus, is assigned with the following tasks –

(i) Specifying and accumulating the input resources, i.e.,

management, men, information, materials, machine and capital.

(ii) Designing and installing the assembly or conversion process to transform the inputs into output, and

(iii) Coordinating and operating the production process so that the desired goods and services may be produced efficiently and at a minimum cost.

SCOPE OF PRODUCTION MANAGEMENT

Production management is mainly associated with the factory management crept with the development of factory system. Before the evolution of factory system, manufacturing activities were carried on by single person that posed no or very insignificant problem of production and therefore question of production management did not arise. But with the inception of factory system, the situation changed and so many problems of production were begun to creep up and necessity arose to tackle with the problems of quality control, layout facilities, meeting the schedules and organization of production activities. Thus the scope of production management began to develop. In early stage, the stress was on controlling the labour costs because labour cost was the major element of the total cost of production. With the continuing development of factory system, the trend towards mechanization and automation developed and it resulted in the increased costs of indirect labour higher than the direct labour costs. So concerns found it difficult to run the business in these circumstances and evolved many controlling devices to regulate the cost of production. They had developed devices like designing and packing of products, indirect labour cost control, production & inventory control and quality control. Since the level of production has increased tremendously, so many other production problems have been added to its scope. In the present era of intense competition, the scope of production management is very wide. The production department in an enterprise is not only concerned with the full exploitation of production facilities but also the human factor that indirectly affects the production, utilization of latest techniques of production and the production of quality goods to the satisfaction of customers of the product. The various activities that form scope of production function can be studied in the following broad areas –

1. *Product Selection and Design* : The product mix

makes the production system either efficient or inefficient. Choosing the right products, keeping the mission and overall objectives of the organization in mind is the key to success. Design of the product, which gives it enough functional and aesthetic value, is of paramount importance. It is the design of the product which makes the organization competitive or noncompetitive. Value engineering does help to retain enough features, while eliminating the unnecessary ones.

2. *Activities Relating to Production System Designing :* Decision related to the production system design is one of the most important activity of the production management. This activity is related to production engineering and includes problems regarding design of tools and jigs, the design, development and installation of equipment and the selection of the optimum size of the firm. All these areas require the technical expertise on the part of the production manager and his staff.

3. *Facilities Location:* The selection of an optimum plant location very much depends upon the decision taken regarding production engineering. A wrong decision

may prove disastrous. Location should as far as possible cut down the production and distribution cost. There are diverse factors to be considered for selecting the location of a plant.

4. *Method Study* : The next decision regarding production system design concerns the use of those techniques which are concerned with work environment and work measurement. Standard methods should be devised for performing the repetitive functions efficiently. Unnecessary movements should be eliminated and suitable positioning of the workers for different processes should be developed. Such methods should be devised with the help of time study and motion study. The workers should be trained accordingly.

5. *Facilities Layout and Materials Handling* : Plant layout deals with the arrangements of machines and plant facilities. The machines should be so arranged that the flow of production remains smooth. There should not be overlapping, duplication or interruption in production flow. Product layout, where machines are arranged in a sequence required for the processing

of a particular product, and process layout, where machines performing the similar processes are grouped together are two popular methods of layout. The departments are laid out in such a way that the cost of material handling is reduced. There should be proper choice of materials handling equipment. These days, computer software is available for planning the process layout (e.g. CRAFT, CORELAP etc.). Group Technology (G.T.), Cellular Manufacturing Systems (CMS) and Flexible Manufacturing Systems (FMS) have made our concepts of layout planning undergo a tremendous change.

6. *Capacity Planning :* This deals with the procurement of productive resources. Capacity refers to a level of output of the conversion process over a period of time. Full capacity indicates maximum level of output. Capacity is planned for short-term as well as for long term. Process industries pose challenging problems in capacity planning, requiring in the long run, expansion and contraction of major facilities in the conversion process. Some tools that help us in capacity planning are marginal costing (Break Even Analysis), learning

curves, linear programming, and decision trees.

7. *Production Planning* : The decisions in production planning include preparation of short-term production schedules, plan for maintaining the records of raw materials, finished and semi-finished stock, specifying how the production resources of the concern are to be employed over some future time in response to the predicted demand for products and services. Production planning takes a given product or line of products and organizes in advance the manpower, materials, machines and money required for a predetermined output in a given period of time.

Thus, production planning is a management technique which attempts to gain the best utilization of a firm's manufacturing facilities. It is gained by the integration and coordination of the manpower, machines, materials and plant services employed in the manufacturing cycle.

8. *Production control* : After planning, the next managerial production function is to control the production according to the production plans because production plans cannot be activated unless they are

properly guided and controlled. For this purpose, production manager has to regulate work assignment, review work process, check and remove discrepancies, if any, in the actual and planned performances.

According to Soriegel and Lansburgh "Production control is the process of planning production in advance of operations; establishing the exact route of each individual item, part or assembly; setting, starting and finishing dates for each important item, assembly and the finished products; and releasing the necessary orders as well as initiating the required follow-up to effect the smooth functioning of the enterprise".

Thus production control involves the following stages :

(i) Planning — setting targets of production.

(ii) Routing — to decide the route or flow-of production activity.

(iii) Dispatching — to issue materials and authorizations for the use of machines and plant services.

(iv) Follow-up — it compares the actual production with the targeted production. Deviations are found out and corrected and reasons are investigated.

9. *Inventory Control :* Inventory control deals with the control over raw-materials, work-in-progress, finished products, stores, supplies, tools, and so is included in production management.

The raw materials, supplies etc. should be purchased at right time, of right quality, in right quantity, from right source and at right price. This five 'R's consideration enables the scientific purchases.

Store-keeping is also an important aspect of inventory control. The raw materials, work-in-progress, finished goods, supplies, tools etc. should be stored efficiently. The different levels of inventory should be managed properly and the issue of materials to departments should be made promptly and effectively. Proper records should also be kept for various items of inventory control.

The production manager has to look after the inventory control activities at three levels –

(i) Control of inventories such as raw materials,

purchased parts, finished goods and supplies through the inventory control technique;

(ii) Control of flow of materials into the plants through the technique of judicious purchasing;

(iii) Control of work-in-progress through production control.

10. *Quality control :* The other important decision taken by the production manager concerns quality control. Product quality refers to the composite product characteristics of engineering and manufacturing that determines the degree to which the product in use will meet the expectations of the customers. Quality control can be ensured through the techniques of inspection and statistical quality control.

11. *Maintenance and Replacement :* In this we cover preventive methods to avoid machine break-downs, maintenance, policies regarding repair and replacement decisions. Maintenance manpower is to be scheduled and repair jobs are to be sequenced. There are some preventive replacements also. Machine condition is to be constantly monitored. Effective maintenance is a crucial problem for India

which can help better capacity utilization and make operations systems productive enough.

12. *Cost Reduction and Control :* Cost reduction ultimately improves productivity. The industry becomes competitive. Essentially cost reduction and cost elimination are productivity techniques. Value engineering, budgetary control, standard costing, cost control of labour and materials etc. help to keep costs optimal.

All Production decisions are subject to control measures, after receiving proper feed-back. Control function is exercised over the quantity to be produced, quality expected, time needed, inventory consumed & carried and costs incurred. Control system is designed after due cost benefit analysis. Controls should be selective. A self-controlling cybernetic system though preferable is not possible in all complex industries.

Environmental changes ultimately affect all the systems of the organization. A dynamic environment makes it compulsory to adapt the production system to the changes in technology and other factors of the environment. Product mix, composition of products, introduction of new products, changing the layout system is some of the representative decisions which respond to environmental feedback.

Apart from these factors, the production system designer should pay full attention to two other important problems, viz. (i) human factor, i.e., the impact of production systems on the workers operating it and (ii) research and development activities. These two problems have a vital impact on production system designing.

Brief History of Production Management

If we assess the past, covering a period of 200 years after Adam Smith, it can be observed that total production capacity as well as productivity have expanded considerably. Production Management has become an empirical applied science. Undoubtedly, during this period, we have responded to the expansion of markets and large scale business units by using the concepts of division of labour and progressive mechanisation in order to achieve economies of large scale production. The history of production management can be studied as under :

Individual Efficiency

Fredric W. Taylor studied the simple output-to-time

relationship for manual labour such as brick-laying. This formed the precursor of the present day 'time-study'. Around the same time, Frank Gilberth and his learned wife Lillian Gilberth examined the motions of the limbs of the workers (such as the hands, legs, eyes, etc.) in performing the jobs, and tried to standardize these motions into certain categories and utilize the classification to arrive at standards for time required to perform a given job. This was the precursor to the present day 'motion study'. Although, to this day Gilberth's classification of movements is used extensively, there have been various modifications and newer classifications.

Collective Efficiency

So far the focus was on controlling the work-output of the manual labourer or the machine operator. The primary objective of production management was that of efficiency-efficiency of the individual operator. The aspects of collective efficiency came into being later, expressed through the efforts of scientists such as Gantt who shifted the attention to scheduling of the operations. (Even now, we use the Gantt Charts in operations scheduling). The considerations of efficiency in the use of materials followed later. It was almost 1930, before a basic inventory model was presented by F. W. Harris.

Quality Control

After the progress of application of scientific principles to the manufacturing aspects, thought progressed to control over the quality of the finished material itself. So far, the focus was on the quantitative aspects; now it shifted to the quality aspects. 'Quality', which is an important customer service objective, came to be recognized for scientific analysis. The analysis of productive systems, therefore, now also included the 'effectiveness' in addition to efficiency. In 1931, Walter Shewart came up with his theory regarding Control Charts for quality or what is known as 'process control'. These charts suggested a simple graphical methodology to monitor the quality characteristics of the output and to control it by exercising control over the process. In 1935, H.F., Dodge, and H.G. Romig came up with the application of statistical principles to the acceptance and/or rejection of the consignments supplied by the suppliers to exercise control over the quality. This field, which has developed over the years, is now known as 'acceptance sampling'.

Effectiveness as a Function of Internal Climate

In addition to effectiveness for the customer, the concept of effectiveness as a function of internal climate dawned on management scientists through the Hawthorne experiments which actually had the purpose of increasing the efficiency of the individual worker. These experiments showed that worker efficiency went up when the intensity of illumination was gradually increased, and even when the intensity of illumination was gradually decreased, the worker efficiency still kept rising. This puzzle could be explained only through the angle of human psychology; the very fact that somebody cared, mattered much to the workers who gave increased output. Till now; it was Taylor's theory of elementalization of task and thus the specialization in one task which found much use in Henry Ford's Assembly Line.

Advent of Operations Research Techniques

The application of scientific techniques in management really received a big boost during the World War II period when the field of Operations Research came into being. During this war, the Allied Force took the help of statisticians, scientists, engineers, etc. to analyze and answer, questions such as : What is the optimum way of mining the harbours of the areas occupied by the Japanese? What should be the optimum size of the fleet of the supply ships, taking into account the costs of loss due to enemy attack and the costs of employing the defence fleet? Such research about the military operations was termed as Operations Research. After World War II, this field was further investigated and developed by academic institutions; and today, it has become one of the very important fields of management theory. Various techniques such as Linear Programming, Mathematical Programming, Game Theory, Queuing Theory, etc. developed by people such as George Dantzig. A. Charnes, W. W. Cooper, etc. have become indispensable tools for management decision-making today.

The Computer Era

After the breakthrough made by Operations Research, another marvel came into being the Computer. Around 1955, IBM developed the digital computer and made it available later on a large-scale basis. This made possible the complex and repeated computations involved in various Operations Research and other Management Science techniques, and definitely added to the spread of the use of Management Science concepts and techniques in all fields of decision-making.

The Production and Operations Management Scenario Today

More importantly, the long experience of industrial life, the growth of technology and the rapidly growing availability of its benefits, have all been changing the value systems all over the world. The concepts of 'quality of life', whether expressed explicitly or otherwise, have gained solid ground. The demand for 'service' or the 'state' utility is fast catching up with the demand for 'form' utility. Services are becoming as important, if not more, as the availability of physical products. The demand for 'variety' in products and services is on the increase. The concepts of 'customer' and 'customer orientation' are very vital today, as also the definition of the word 'customer' itself. The producing workers themselves are a part of the 'customers'. There is great pressure every where to enhance the quality of life in general. If in the developed countries there is an increased demand for 'flexi-time' (flexible times of working), in India we have already witnessed the shortening of the traditional six-day week to a five-day week in even traditional organizations such as the Central Government and State Governments. (Of course, the total time of working has remained the same.) In addition to all this, there is the increasing complexity of the space-age economies, the socio-techno-economic scene and the problem of depleting resources. Such a complex scenario needs freedom from compartmentalized thinking and an integrated consideration of the various factors that impinge on the production and operations management system. It needs to introduce fresh variables, e.g. that of safety in the external and internal environment and an added emphasis on maintenance. These are the challenges of the production and operations management discipline.

Production Administration

Production is a succession of work elements applied to natural materials with the purpose of transforming these into desired goods and services for the satisfaction of human wants. Thus modem production phenomenon is an evolution and production administration deals with planning and control of various operations and components associated with production process. However there are a number of definitions given by different experts of Production administration according to their own experiences. The concept can be explained by the following definitions :

According to Frederick W. Taylor, father of scientific management, "functional management consists of division of management work in such a way that every person below the rank of assistant superintendent has as few responsibilities as possible. If possible the work of each man should be confined to perform a single leading function".

The various departments of Production Administration can be listed as production engineering, production planning and production control.

ORGANISATIONAL CHART OF PRODUCTION MANAGEMENT

DEPARTMENT

Managing Director

Works Manager

Managers of Various Production Departments

| A | B | C | D | E |

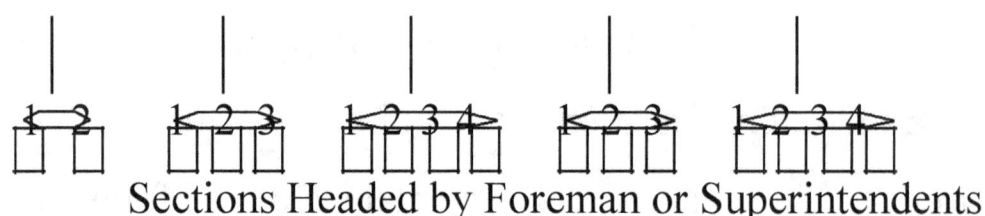

Sections Headed by Foreman or Superintendents

Many pioneers in the field of management namely Oliver, Sheldon, Gantt etc. limited the scope of production administration to planning and implementation

LESSON : 2

TYPES OF PRODUCTION SYSTEMS AND PLANT LOCATION

SYSTEM

A system is a logical arrangement of components designed to achieve particular objectives according to a plan. According to Webster, "System is a regularly interacting inter-dependent group of items forming a unified whole". A system may have many components and variation in one component is likely to affect the other components of the system e.g. change in rate of production will affect inventory, overtime hours etc. Production system is the framework within which the production activities of an organization are carried out. At one end of system are inputs and at the other end output. Input and output are linked by certain processes or operations or activities imparting value to the inputs. These processes, operations or activities may be called production systems. The nature of production system may differ from company to company or from plant to plant in the same firm.

Elements of Production System

(i) *Inputs :* Inputs are the physical and human resources

utilised in the production process. They consist of raw materials, parts, capital equipments, human efforts etc.

(ii) *onversion Process :* It refers to a series of operations which are performed on materials and parts.

(iii) Outputs : Outputs are the prodl1; acts or completed parts resulting from the conversion process. Output generates revenue.

(iv) Storage : Storage take place after the receipt of inputs, between one operation and the other and after the output.

(v) Transportation : Inputs are transported from one operation to another in the production process.

(vi) Information : It provides system control through measurement, comparison, feedback, and corrective action.

Types of Production Systems

There are two main types of production systems : (i) Continuous System (ii) Intermittent System

i) Flow or Continuous System : According to Buffa, "Continuous flow production situations are those where the facilities are standardised as to routings and flow since inputs are standardised. Therefore a standard set of processes and sequences of process can be adopted". Thus continuous or flow production refers to the manufacturing of large quantities of a single or at most a very few varieties of products with a standard set of processes and sequences. The mass production is carried on continuously for stock in anticipation of demand.

Characteristics :

(i) The volume of output is generally large (mass production) and goods are produced in anticipation of demand.

(ii) The product design and the operations sequence are standardised i.e identical products are produced.

(iii) Special purpose automatic machines are used to perform standardised operations.

(iii) Machine capacities are balanced so that materials are fed at one end of the process and finished product is received at the other end.

(iv) Fixed path materials handling equipment is used due to the predetermined sequence of operations.

(v) Product layout designed according to a separate line for each product is considered.

Merits

(i) The main advantage of continuous system is that work-in-progress inventory is minimum.

(ii) The quality of output is kept uniform because each stage develops skill through repetition of work.

(iii) Any delay at any stage is automatically detected.

(iv) Handling of materials is reduced due to the set pattern of production line. Mostly the materials are handled through conveyer belts, roller conveyers, pipe lines, overhead cranes etc.

(v) Control over materials, cost and output is simplified.

(vi) The work can be done by semi-skilled workers because of their specialization.

Demerits : Continuous system, however, is very rigid and if there is a fault in one operation the entire process is disturbed. Due to continuous flow, it becomes necessary to avoid piling up of work or any blockage on the line. Unless the fault is cleared immediately, it will force the preceding as well as the subsequent stages to be stopped. Moreover, it is essential to maintain stand-by equipments to meet any breakdowns resulting in production stoppages. Thus investments in machines are fairly high.

Continuous production is of the following types :

(a) *Mass Production* : Mass production refers to the manufacturing of standardised parts or components on a large scale. Mass production system offers economies of scale as the volume of output is large. Quality of products tends to be uniform and high due to standardisation and mechanisation. In a properly designed and equipped process, individual expertise plays a less prominent role.

(b) *Process Production* : Production is carried on continuously through a uniform and standardised sequence of operations. Highly sophisticated and automatic machines are used. Process production is employed in bulk processing of certain materials. The typical processing Industries are fertilizers plants, petrochemical plants and milk dairies which have highly automated systems and sophisticated controls. They are not labour-intensive and the worker is just an operator to monitor the system and take corrective steps if called for.

On the basis of the nature of production process, flow production may be classified into *Analytical and Synthetic Production.*

In *Analytical Process* of production, a raw material is broken into different products e.g. crude oil is analysed into gas, naptha, petrol etc. Similarly, coal is processed to obtain coke, coal gas, coal tar etc.

Synthetic Process of production involves the mixing of two or more materials to manufacture a product for instance, lauric acid, myristic acid, stearic acid are synthesised to manufacture soap.

(c) *Assembly Lines* : Assembly line a type of flow production which is developed in the automobile industry in the USA. A manufacturing unit prefers to develop and employ assembly line because it helps to improve the efficiency of production. In an assembly line, each machine must directly receive material from the previous machine and pass it directly to the next machine. Machine and equipment should be arranged in such a manner that every operator has a free and safe access to each machine. Space should be provided for free movement of fork lifts, trucks etc. which deliver materials and collect finished products.

(ii) Intermittent Production System

According to Buffa, "Intermittent situations are those

where the facilities must be flexible enough to handle a variety of products and sizes or where the basic nature of the activity imposes change of important characteristics of the input (e.g. change. in the product design). In instances such as these, no single sequence pattern of operations is appropriate, so the relative location of the operation must be a compromise that is best for all inputs considered together". In the industries following the intermittent production system, some components may be made for inventory but they are combined differently for different customers. The finished product is heterogenous but within a range of standardized options assembled by the producers. Since production is partly for stock and partly for consumer demand, there are problems to be met in scheduling, forecasting, control and coordination.

Characteristics :

(i)   The flow of production is intermittent, not continuous.

(ii) The volume of production is generally small.

(iii) A wide variety of products are produced.

(iv) General purpose, machines and equipments are used so as to be adaptable to a wide variety of operations.

(v) No single sequence of operations is used and periodical adjustments are made to suit different jobs or batches.

(vi) Process layout is most suited.

Intermittent system is much more complex than continuous production because every product has to be treated differently under the constraint of limited resources. Intermittent system can be -effective in situations which satisfy the following conditions :

(i) The production centres should be located in such a manner so that they can handle a wide range of inputs.

(ii) Transportation facilities between production centres should be flexible enough to accommodate variety of routes for different inputs.

(iii) It should be provided with necessary storage facility.

Intermittent Production May be of two types :

(a) **Job Production :** Job or unit production involves the manufacturing of single complete unit with the use of a group of operators and process as per the customer's order. This is a 'special order' type of production. Each job or product is different from the other and no repetition is involved. The product is usually costly and non-standardised. Customers do not make demand for exactly the same product on a continuing basis and therefore production becomes intermittent. Each product is a class by itself and constitutes a separate job for production process. Ship building, electric power plant, dam construction etc. are common examples of job production.

Characteristics :

(i) The product manufactured is custom-made or non-standardised.

(ii) Volume of output is generally small.

(iii) Variable path materials handling equipment are used.

(iv) A wide range of general purpose machines like grinders, drilling, press, shaper etc. is used.

Merits :

It is flexible and can be adopted easily to changes in product design. A fault in one operation does not result into complete stoppage of the process. Besides it is cost effective and time-effective since the nature of the operations in a group are similar. There is reduced material handling since machines are close in a cell. The waiting period between operations is also reduced. This also results in a reduced work-in-progress inventory.

Demerits :

Job shop manufacturing is the most complex system of production e.g. in building a ship thousands of individual parts must be fabricated and assembled. A complex schedule of activities is required to ensure smooth flow of work without any bottlenecks. Raw materials and work-in-progress inventories are high due to uneven and irregular flow of work. Work loads are unbalanced, speed of work is slow and unit costs are high.

(b) ***Batch Production :*** It is defined as "The manufacture of a product in small or large batches or lots at intervals by a series of operations, each operation being carried out on the whole batch before any subsequent operation is performed". The batch production is a mixture of mass production and job production. Under it machines turn out different products at intervals, each product being produced for comparatively short time using mass production methods.

Both job production and batch production are similar in nature, except that in batch production the quantity of product manufactured is comparatively large.

Demerits :

Work-in-progress inventory is high and large storage space is required. Due to frequent changes in product design no standard sequence of operation can be used. Machine set-ups and tooling arrangements have to be changed frequently. The main problem in batch production is the idle time between one operation and the other. The work has to wait until a particular operation is carried out on the whole batch.

Comparison of Different Production Systems

As we have discussed various systems and sub-systems in detail in the above lines, we can now make a comparative study of them as follows :

(i) Manufacturing Cost : Cost of production per unit is lowest in process production while it is highest in job production because large scale continuous production is carried out under process production. Unit cost in mass production is higher than the process production while it is lower than the batch production or job production.

(ii) Size and Capital Investment : As stated earlier, the scale of operation is small in job production, medium in

batch production, large in mass production and very large in process production. Hence the size of capital investment differs from system to system. Process production calls for the higher investment while mass production requires lesser amount of capital investment. It is lower in case of job production and comparatively higher in batch production.

(iii) Flexibility in Production : In case of change in demand of the product, the production facilities may be adjusted very shortly without increasing much expenses under the system of job or batch production. But both the sub-systems of continuous production system i.e., mass production or process production employ single purpose machine in their manufacturing processes. They cannot adjust their production facilities so quickly and easily as is possible in job or batch production where general purpose machines are used.

(iv) Required Technical Ability : Both job and batch production require high skilled technical foreman and other executives. But under mass production for process production systems, managerial ability plays an important role because it require higher ability for planning and coordinating several functions in mass and process

production than in the case of job and batch production.

(v) Organisational Structure : Mostly functional organisation is adopted in case of job and batch production systems. On the other hand, divisional organisation is preferred in mass and product process production systems due to the greater emphasis for centralisation.

Job Security : Job and batch systems of production do not provide and type of job security to workers due to their intermittent character. During odd times, workers particularly unskilled workers are thrown out of job. On the contrary, mass and process production systems provide greater job security to workers because production operations are carried out continuously in anticipation of stable and continuous demand of the product.

(vii) Industrial Application : The application of different systems is suitable in different industries depending upon the nature of work. The mechanism of job production applies in products of construction and manufacturing industries like buildings, bridges, special purpose machines etc. Batch production is mostly used in mechanical engineering and consumer-goods industries like cotton, jute, machine tools, shoe-making etc. Mass production is

found in automobiles, sugar refining, refrigerators, electrical goods etc. Process production is most appropriate in chemical, petroleum, milk processing industries etc.

Thus, a comparative view of the different systems of production reveals that no one system is suitable for all types of industries and therefore each system is different in itself and must be studied with reference to the nature of industry.

PLANT LOCATION

Plant : A plant is a place, where men, materials, money, machinery etc. are brought together for manufacturing products. The objective of minimisation of cost of production can be achieved only when the plant is of the right size and at a right place where economies of all kinds in production are available. The planning for 'where' to locate the operations facilities should start from 'what' are organization's objectives, priorities, goals and the strategies required to achieve the same in the general socio-economic-techno-business-legal environment currently available and expected to be available in the long-term future. Unless the objectives and priorities of an organization are clear i.e. the general direction is clear, effective functional or composite strategies cannot be designed. And, it is these strategies of which the location design is a product.

Different Situations for Plant Location Decision

(i) *To select a proper geographic region :* The organizational objectives alongwith the various long-term considerations about marketing, technology, internal organizational strengths and weaknesses, region specific resources and business environment, legal-governmental environment, social environment and geographical environment suggest a suitable region for locating the operations facility.

(ii) *Selecting a specific site within the region :* Once the suitable region is identified, the next problem is that of choosing the best site from an available set. Choice of a site is much less dependent on the organization's long-term strategies. It is more a question of evaluating alternative sites for their tangible and intangible costs if the operations were located there. Cost economies now figure prominently at this final stage of facilities-location problem.

(iii) *Location choice for the first time :* In this case, there

is no prevailing strategy to which one needs to confirm. However, the organizational strategies have to be first decided upon before embarking upon the choice of the location of the operating facility/facilities. The importance of the long-term strategies can not be over emphasized. Cost economics are always important but not at the cost of long-term business/ organizational objectives.

(iv) ***Location choice for an ongoing organization :*** A new plant has to fit into multi-plant operations strategy as discussed below :

(a) *Plant Manufacturing Distinct Products or Product Lines*

This strategy is necessary where the needs of technological and resource inputs are specialized fir distinctively different for the different products/product-lines. For example, a high quality precision product-line should preferably not be located along with other product-line requiring little emphasis on precision. It may not be proper to have too many contradictions such as sophisticated and old equipment, highly skilled and not so skilled personnel, delicate processes and those that could permit rough handling, all under one roof and one set of managers. Such a setting leads to much confusion regarding the required emphasis and the management policies. Product specialization may be necessary in a highly competitive market; it may also be necessary in order to fully exploit the special resource potential of a particular geographical area. Instances of product specialization could be many : A watch manufacturing unit and a machine tools unit; a textile unit and a sophisticated organic chemical unit; an injectible pharmaceuticals unit and a consumer products unit; etc. All these pairs have to be distinctively different-in technological sophistication, in process, and in the relative stress on certain aspects of management. The more decentralised these pairs are in terms of the management and in terms of their physical location, the better would be the planning and control and the utilization of the resources.

(b) Manufacturing Plants Each supplying to a Specific Market Area

Here, each plant manufactures almost all of the company's product. This type of strategy is useful where market proximity consideration dominates the resources and technology considerations. This strategy requires a great deal of coordination from the corporate office. An extreme example of this strategy is that of soft-drinks bottling plants.

(c) *Manufacturing Plants Divided According to the Product/Product Line being Manufactured; and these Special-Product Plants Located in Various Market Areas.*

(d) *Plants Divided on the Basic of the Processes or Stages in Manufacturing*

Each production process or stage of manufacturing may require distinctively different equipment capabilities, labour skills, technologies, and managerial policies and emphasis. Since the products of one plant feed into the other plant, this strategy requires much centralized coordination of the manufacturing activities from the corporate office who are expected to understand the various technological and resources nuances of all the plants. Sometimes such a strategy is used because of the defence/national security considerations. For instance, the Ordnance Factories in India.

(e) *Plants Emphasizing Flexibility in Adapting to*

Constantly Changing Product Needs

This needs much coordination between plants to meet the changing needs and at the same time ensure efficient use of the facilities and resources. The new plant or branch-facility has to fit into the organization's existing strategy, mainly because the latter has been the product of deep thinking about the long-term prospects and problems, and strengths and weaknesses for the organization as a whole.

Factors Affecting Plant Location Decisions

Hardly there is any location which can be ideal or perfect. One has to strike a balance between various factors affecting plant location. Some factors are crucial in deciding the location of the plant while some other factors are less important. In taking the decision of location of plant, due regard should be given to minimisation of cost of production & distribution and maximisation of profit. The decision of plant location should be based on nine M's, namely money, material, manpower, market, motive power, management, machinery, means of communication and momentum to an early start. The following are some of the important factors which the management must carefully bear in mind in selecting an optimum site for the plant :

(i) *Nearness to Raw Material :* It will reduce the cost of transporting raw material from the vendor's end to the plant. Especially those plants which consume raw material in bulk, or raw material is heavy weight, must be located close to the source of raw material. If the raw materials are perishable, the plant is to be located near the source of material. This is true of fruit canning industry. Sugar and paper and other industries using weight losing materials are also located near point of supply. Industries which depend for their raw materials on other industries tend to be located near such industries e.g. the petrochemicals industries are located near refineries. Similarly, Thermal Power Stations are situated near coal mines. In case the raw material are imported, the unit must be established near the port. When a company uses a number of raw materials and their sources are at different location, the ideal site for the plant shall be a place where the transportation costs of various raw materials are the minimum. Apart from these considerations, a promoter must view the supply of raw materials from the following angles also :

(a) If supply of raw materials is linked with finance, it must be set up where the raw material is available at reduced or concessional rates.

(b) Reliability and continuity of the source of supply, and

(c) The security of means of transport.

(ii) *Nearness to Markets :* It reduces the cost of transportation as well as the chances of the finished products getting damaged and spoiled in the way. Moreover a plant being near to the market can catch a big share of the market and can render quick service to the customers. Industries producing perishable or fragile commodities are also attracted towards the market because of savings in time and transportation costs. Industrial units have a tendency to disperse if they find a new market for their products.

(iii) Availability of Labour : Stable labour force, of right kind, of adequate size (number) and at reasonable rates with its proper attitude towards work are a few factors which govern plant location to a major extent. The purpose of the management is to face less bycotts, strikes or lockouts and to achieve lower labour cost per unit of production.

(iv) Availability of Fuel and Power : Because of the wide spread of electric power, in most cases fuel (coal, oil etc.) has not remained a deciding factors for plant location. It is of course essential that electric power should remain available continuously, in proper quantity and at reasonable rates.

(v) Availability of Water : Water is used for processing, as in paper and chemical industries, and is also required for drinking and sanitary purposes. Depending upon the nature of the plant, water should be available in adequate quantity and should be of proper quality (clean and pure). A chemical, fertilizer, thermal power station etc. should not be set-up at a location which IS famous for water shortage.

(vi) *Climatic Conditions :* Climate conditions also influence the location decision. Some industries need special type of climate to run the unit effectively. For example, cotton industry requires a humid climate and therefore it is mainly localised at Bombay, Ahmedabad, etc. But the scientific development and new inventions have lowered down the importance of the factor. So due to the development of artificial humidification, cotton textile industry can now be started in any region of the county. The question of climate is more important for agricultural product like tea, coffee, rubber, cotton etc. even today.

(vii) Government Policy : Certain states give aid as loans, machinery, built up sheds etc. to attract industrialists. In planned economy, Government plays an important role on the location of industry. In India Government follows the policy of balanced regional growth of the country which is very important from the point of view of defence and social problems like slum, disparity of income & wealth and optimum use of resources. In order to implement this policy, Government offers several incentives to entrepreneurs to locate their industrial units in backward regions or no-industry regions. It offers tax concessions or loan facilities or factory sheds at cheaper rates. Sometimes Government announces certain disincentives to industries located at a certain place. Thus Government policy plays an important role in the location of industry.

(viii)Land : The shape of the site, cost, drainage, the

probability of floods, earthquakes (from the past history) etc. influence the selection of plant location.

(ix) *Community Attitude :* Success of Industry depends very much on the attitude of local people and whether they want to work or not.

(xi) *Security :* Considerations like law and order situation, political stability and safety also influence the location decision. No entrepreneur will like to start the industry at a place which is not safe and where there are law and order disturbances off and on.

(xii) *Transport Facilities :* A lot of money is spent both in transporting the raw material and the finished goods. Depending upon the size of raw material and finished goods, a suitable method of transportation like roads, rail, water or air is selected and accordingly the plant location is decided. Transportation costs depend mainly on the weight carried and the distance to be covered. In some industries, weight of the raw material is much higher than that of finished product. e.g. in a weight losing industry like sugar manufacturing four to five tons of sugarcanes have to be carried per ton of sugar. Similarly in Iron and Steel

Industry two tons of iron is required to produce one ton of pig iron. Therefore the transport costs can be saved by locating near the source of materials. In case of weight gaining industry, location near the market may result in savings in transportation costs. e.g. in soft drink the weight of finished product is higher than raw material.

(xiii) *Momentum of an early start :* Another factor of some importance has been the momentum of an early start. Some places got localised only because one or two units of that industry started production there. With the passage of time, these places gained importance and attracted other units of the industry. As a place gains importance, certain facilities usually beg in to develop. For example, (i) transport facilities are developed because railways and other agencies find it economical to serve that centres, (ii) specialised firms start to take up repair and maintenance job for such units, (iii) banking facilities are made available and (iv) labour possessing various skills are attracted there. These facilities further attract more industries.

(xiv) *Personal Factors :* Personal preferences and

prejudices of an entrepreneur also play an important role in the choice of location. Economic consideration do not weight much. For instance, Mr. Ford started cars manufacturing motor in Detroit because it was his home town. It must however, be recognized that such location cannot endure unless they prove to be economical enough in the long run.

(xiv) *Communication Facilities :* Every business firm requires every type of business information regarding the position of labour, market, raw materials and finished goods and this facility is available only when communication facilities are there. As communications facilities are not adequately available in rural areas, industries are very much reluctant to start their business there.

(xv) *Other Considerations :* There are certain other considerations that influence the location decisions which are :

(a) Presence of related Industry

(b) Existence of hospitals, marketing centres, schools, banks, post office, clubs etc.

(c) Local bye-laws, taxes, building ordinances etc.

(d) Facility for expansion

(e) New enterprise owned or operated by a single group of companies should be so located that its work can be integrated with the work of the associated establishments.

(f) Industries like nuclear power stations, processes explosive in nature, chemical process likely to pollute the atmosphere should be located in remote areas.

(g) Historical factors etc.

LESSON : 3

PLANT LAYOUT

MEANING OF PLANT LAYOUT

Plant layout means the disposition of the various facilities (equipments, materials, manpower etc.) within the area of the site selected. Plant layout begins with the design of the factory building and goes up to the location and movement of work. All the facilities like equipments, raw materials, machinery, tools, fixtures, workers etc. are given a proper place. In the words of James Lundy, "It identically involves the allocation of space and the arrangement of equipment in such a manner that overall costs are minimised". According to Mo Naughton Waynel, "A good layout results in comforts, convenience, appearance, safety and profits. A poor layout results in congestion, waste, frustration and inefficiency".

Plant layout is very complex in nature as it involves concepts relating to such fields as engineering, architecture, economics and business administration. Since a plant layout, when properly designed, encompasses all production' and service facilities and provides for the most effective utilization of men, with materials and machines constituting the process, is a master blue print for coordinating all operations.

Objective of a Good Plant Layout

The principal objective of a proper plant layout is to maximize the production at the minimum of the costs. This objective should be kept in mind while designing a layout for a new plant as well as while making the necessary changes in the existing layout in response to changes in management policies and processes and techniques of production. Besides, it must satisfy the needs of all people associated with the production system, i.e. workers, supervisors and managers. If a layout is to fulfil this goal, it should be planned with the following clear objectives in mind :

i) There is the proper utilization of cubic space (Le. length, width and height). Maximum use of volume available should be made. For example, conveyors can be run above head height and used as moving work in progress or tools and equipments can be suspended from the ceiling. The principle is particularly true in stores where goods can be stored at considerable heights without inconvenience.

ii) Waiting time of the semi-finished products is minimised.

iii) Working conditions are safer, better (well ventilated rooms etc.) and improved.

iv) Material handling and transportation is minimised and efficiently controlled. For this, one has to consider the movement distances between different work areas as well as the number of times such movements occur per unit period of time.

v) The movements made by the workers are minimised.

vii) Suitable spaces are allocated to production centres. Plant maintenance is simpler.

viii) There is increased flexibility for changes in product design and for future expansion. It must be capable of incorporating, without major changes, new equipment to meet technological requirements or to eliminate waste.

ix) A good layout permits materials to move through the plant at the desired speed with the lowest cost.

x) There is increased productivity and better product quality with reduced capital cost.

xi) Boosting up employee morale by providing employee

comforts and satisfaction.

xii) The workers should be so arranged that there is no difficulty in supervision, coordination and control. There should be no 'hiding-places' into which goods can be mislaid. Goods – raw materials and ready stocks – must be readily observable at all times. It will reduce the pilferage of material and labour.

It should be noted here that the above stated objectives of plant layout are laudable in themselves, it is often difficult to reconcile all of them in a practical situation. And as such, the highest level of skill and judgement are required to be exercised. For this, close association between the entrepreneurs and experienced engineers is a must.

Types of Plant Layout

There are three basic types of plant layout : (i) Functional or process layout, ii) product or line layout, (iii) stationary layout. However the choice of one or the other type of layout depends upon the machines and techniques used in the production.

(a) *Process Layout :* It is also known as functional layout and is characterised by keeping similar machines or similar operations at one location (place). In other words, separate departments are established for each specialised operation of production and machines relating to that functions are assembled there. For example, all lathe machines will be at one place, all milling machines at another and so on. This type of layout is generally employed for industries engaged in job order production and non-standardised products. The process layout may be illustrated in the diagram given below :

Reciving	Services	Shipping
Milling	Surface	Packaging
Deptt	Deptt.	Finishing
	Assembling	Inspection
	O F I C E S	

Advantages :

i) Wide flexibility exists as regards allotment of work to equipments and workers. The production capacity is not arranged in rigid sequence and fixed rate capacity with line balancing. Alteration or change in sequence of operations can easily be made as and when required without upsetting the existing plant layout plan.

ii) Better quality product, because the supervisors and workers attend to one type of machines and operations.

iii)   Variety of jobs, coming as different job orders make the work more interesting for workers.

iv)   Workers in one section are not affected by the nature of operations carried out in another section. e.g. a lathe operator is not affected by the rays of welding as the two sections are quite separate.

v) Like product layout, the breakdown of one machine does not interrupt the entire production flow.

ii)   This type of layout requires lesser financial investment in machines and equipment because general purpose machines, which are usually of low costs, are used and duplication of machine is avoided. Moreover, general purpose machines do not depreciate or become obsolete as rapidly as specialised machines. It results in lower investment in machines.

iii)   Under process layout, better and efficient supervision is possible because of specialisation in operation.

Disadvantages :

i) Automatic material handling is extremely difficult because fixed material handling equipment like conveyor belt cannot be possible to use.

ii) Completion of same product takes more time.

iii) Raw material has to travel larger distances for getting processed to finished goods. This increases material handling and the associated costs. It is not possible to implement the group incentive schemes on the basis of quantity of the products manufacturing.

iv) This type of layout requires more floor space than the product layout because a distinct department established for each operation.

(vi) Compared to line layout inventory investments are usually higher in case of process layout. It increases the need of working capital in the form of inventory.

(vii) Under process layout, cost of supervision is high because (i) the number of employees per supervisor is less that result in reduced supervisory span of control, and (ii) the work is checked after each operation.

(b) **Product Layout :** It is also known as line (type) layout. It implies that various operations on a product are performed in a sequence and the machines are placed along the product flow line i.e. machines are arranged in the sequence in which a given product will be operated upon. This type of layout is preferred for continuous production i.e. involving a continuous flow of in-process material towards the finished product stage.

Advantages :

i)   Automatic material handling, lesser material handling movements, time and cost.

ii) Product completes in lesser time. Since materials are fed at one end of the layout and finished product is collected at the other end, there is no transportation of raw materials backward and forward. It shortens the manufacturing time because it does not require any time consuming interval transportation till the completion of the process of production. Line balancing may eliminate idle capacity.

iii) Smooth and continuous flow of work. This plan ensures steady flow of production with economy because bottlenecks or stoppage of work at different points of production is got eliminated or avoided due to proper arrangement of machines in sequence.

iv) Less in-process Inventory. The semi-finished product or work-in-progress is the minimum and negligible under this type of layout because the process of production is direct and uninterrupted.

v) Effective quality control with reduced inspection points. It does not require frequent changes in machine set-up. Since production process is integrated and continuous, defective practice can easily be discovered and segregated. This makes inspection easy and economical.

vi) Maximum use of space due to straight production flow and reduced need of interim storing.

vii) *Disadvantages :*

i) Since the specific product determines the layout, a change in product involves major changes in layout and thus the layout flexibility is considerably reduced.

ii) The pace or rate of working depends upon the output rate of the slowest machine. This involves excessive idle time for other machines if the production line is not adequately balanced.

iii) Machines being scattered along the line, more

machines of each type have to be purchased for helping a few as stand by, because if one machine in the line fails, it may lead to shut down of the complete production line.

iv) It is difficult to increase production beyond the capacities of the production lines.

v) As the entire production is the result of the joint efforts of all operations in the line, it is difficult to implement individual incentive schemes.

vi) Since there are no separate departments for various types of work, supervision is also difficult.

vii) Under this system, labour cost is high because (a) absenteeism may create certain problems because every worker is specialist in his own work or he specialises on a particular machine. In order to avoid the bottleneck, surplus workers who are generalists and can be fitted on a number of machines will have to be employed; (b) monotony is another problem with the workers. By doing the work of repetitive nature along assembly line, they feel bore (c) as machines play the dominant role in production under this system, workers have no opportunity to demonstrate their talent; (d) noise, vibrations, temperature, moisture, gas etc. may cause health hazards. In this way, labour costs are high.

It is now quite clear from the above discussion that both the systems have their own merits and demerits. Advantages of one type of layout are generally the disadvantages of other type. Thus with a view to securing the advantage of both the systems a combined layout may be designed.

(c) Static Product Layout or Project Layout or Stationary Layout

The manufacturing operations require the movements of men, machines, and materials, in the product layout and process layout generally the machines are fixed installations and the operators are static in terms of their specified work stations. It is only the materials which move from operation to operation for the purpose of processing. But where the product is large in size and heavy in weight, it tends to be static e.g. ship building. In such a production system, the product remains static and men and machines move performing the operations on the product.

Advantages of stationary Layout : The advantages of this type of layout are as under :

1. *Flexible :* This layout is fully flexible and is capable of absorbing any sort of change in product and process. The project can be completed according to the needs of the customers and as per their specification.

2. *Lower labour cost :* People are drawn from functional departments. They move back to their respective departments as soon as the work is over. This is economical, if a number of orders are at hand and each one is in a different stage of progress. Besides, one or two workers can be assigned to a project from start to finish. Thus it reduces labour cost.

3. *Saving in time :* The sequence of operations can be changed if some materials do not arrive or if some people are absent. Since the job assignment is so long, different sets of people operate simultaneously on the same assignment doing different operations.

4. *Other benefits :* (i) It requires less floor space because machines and equipment are in moving position and there is no need of fixing them. (ii) This arrangement is most suitable way of assembling large and heavy products.

Disadvantages of stationary layout : The disadvantages of this type of layout are :

(i) *Higher capital investment :* Compared to product or process layout, capital investment is higher in this type of layout. Since a number of assignments are taken, investment in materials, men and machines is made at a higher cost.

(ii) *Unsuitability :* This type of layout is not suitable for manufacturing or assembling small products in large quantities. It is suitable only in case where the product is big or the assembling process is complex.

Factors influencing Plant Layout

The following are some important factors which influence the planning of effective layout to a significant degree.

1. *Nature of the product :* The nature of product to be manufactured will significantly affect the layout of the plant. Stationary layout will be most suitable for heavy products while line layout will be best for the manufacture of light products because small and light products can be moved from one machine to another very easily and, therefore, more attention can be paid to machine locations and handling of materials.

2. *Volume of Production :* Volume of production and the standardisation of the product also affect the type of layout. If standardised commodities are to be manufactured on large scale, line type of layout may be adopted. If production is made on the order of the customers, the functional layout is better to be adopted.

3. *Basic managerial policies and decisions :* The type of layout depends very much on the decisions and policies of the management to be followed in producing a commodity with regard to size of plant , kind and quality of the product; scope for expansion to be provided for, the extent to which the plant is to be integrated, amount of stocks to be carried at any time, the kind of employee facilities to be provided etc.

4. *Nature of plant location :* The size, shape and topography of the site at which plant is located will naturally affect the type of layout to be followed in view of the maximum utilisation of space available. For example, if a site is near the railway line the arrangement of general layout for receiving and shipping and for the best flow of production in and out

the plant may be made by the side of railway line. If space is narrow and the production process is lengthy, the layout of plant may be arranged on the land surface in the following manner :

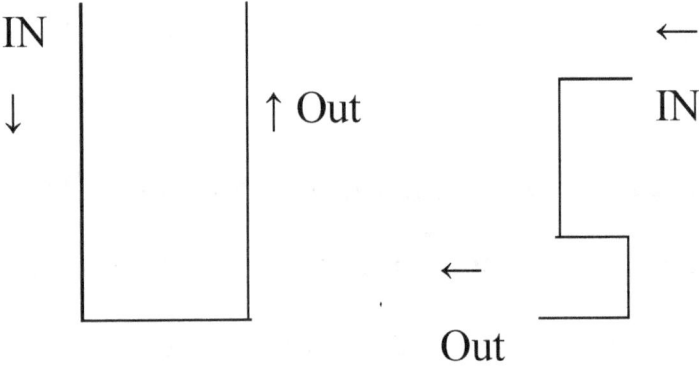

5. *Type of industry process :* This is one of the most important factors influencing the choice of type of plant layout. Generally the types of layout particularly the arrangement of machines and work centres and the location of workmen varies according to the nature of the industry to which the plant belongs. For the purpose of layout, industry may be classified into two broad categories :

(i) intermittent and (ii) continuous. Intermittent type of industries are those which manufacture different components or different machines. Such industries may manufacture the parts, when required according to the market needs. Examples of such industries are shipbuilding plants. In this type of industry functional layout may be the best. The second type of industry in 'continuous' industry. In this type of industry raw materials are fed at one end and the finished goods are received at another end. A continuous industry may either be analytical or synthetical. As analytical industry breaks up the raw material into several parts during the course of production process or changes its form, e.g. oil and sugar refineries. A synthetic industry, on the other hand mixes the two or more materials to manufacture one product alongwith the process of production or assembles several parts to get finished product. Cement and automobile industries are examples of such industry. Line layout is more suitable in continuous process industries.

6. *Types of methods of production :* Layout plans may be different according to the method of production proposed to be adopted. Any of the following three methods may be adopted for production – (i) Job order production, (ii) batch production, and (iii) Mass Production. Under job production goods are produced

according to the orders of the customers and therefore, specifications vary from customer to customer and the production cannot be standardised. The machines and equipment can be arranged in a manner to suit the need of all types of customers. Batch production carries the production of goods in batches or groups at intervals. In this type of manufacturing the product is standardised and production is made generally in anticipation of sales. In such cases functional or process layout may be adopted. In case of mass production of standardised goods, line layout is most suitable form of plant layout.

7. *Nature of machines* : Nature of machines and equipment also affects the layout of plant. If machines are heavy in weight or creates noisy atmosphere, stationary layout may reasonably be adopted. Heavy machines are generally fixed on the ground floor. Ample space should be provided for complicated machines to avoid accidents.

8. *Climate* : Sometimes, temperature, illumination and air are the deciding factors in deciding the location of machines and their establishments. For example, in

lantern manufacturing industry, the spray painting room is built along the factory wall to ensure the required temperature control and air expulsion and then the process of spray painting may be undertaken.

9. *Nature of Materials* : Design and specifications of materials, physical and chemical properties of materials, quantity and quality of materials and combination of materials are probably the most important factors to be considered in planning a layout. So, materials storage and materials handling should be given due consideration. For materials storage factors such as rate of consumption of raw materials, space, volume and weight of raw materials, floor load capacity, ceiling height method of storing should be given special consideration. This will affect the space and the efficiency of the production process in the plant. It will facilitate economic production goods and prompt materials flow and a soundly conceived materials handling system.

10. *Type of machine and equipment* : Machines and equipment may be either general purpose or special purpose. In addition certain tools are used. The

requirements of each machine and equipment are quite different in terms of their space, speed and material handling process and these factors should be given proper consideration while choosing out a particular type of layout. It should also be considered that each machine and equipment is used to its fullest capacity because machines involve a huge investment. For instance, under product layout, certain machines may not be used to their full capacity so care should be taken to make full use of the capacity of the machine and equipment.

11. *Human factor and working conditions :* Man is the most important factor of production and therefore special consideration for their safety and comforts should be given while planning a layout, specific safety items like obstruction-free floor, workers not exposed to hazards, exit etc. should be provided for. The layout should also provide for the comforts to the workers such as provision of rest rooms, drinking water, lavatory and other services etc. Sufficient space is also to be provided for free movement of workers. For this, provisions of Factories Act should be

followed strictly.

12. *Characteristics of the building :* Shape of building, covered and open area, number of storeys, facilities of elevators; parking area, storing place and so on also influence the layout plan. In most of the cases where building is hired, layout is to be adjusted within the space available in the building. Although miner modifications may be done to suit the needs of the plant and equipment. But if new building is to be constructed, proper care should be given to construct it according to the layout plan drawn by experts. Special type of construction is needed to accommodate huge or technical or complex or sophisticated machines and equipment.

It is clear from the above description that several factors are considered while choosing out a plan for plant layout because they affect the production and its cost to a great extent.

Costs Associated With Plant Layout

The costs associated with a decision on plant layout are :

(i) Cost of movement of materials from one work area to another.

(ii) Cost of space.

(iii) Cost of production delay, if any, which are indirect costs.

(iv) Cost of spoilage of materials, if any, when the materials are stacked or stored in conditions which deteriorate the quality of the material.

(v) Cost of labour dissatisfaction and health risks.

(vi) Cost of changes required, if the operational conditions change in the future. This is a long-term cost.

A good layout should minimize all these costs put together.

Techniques of Plant Layout

In designing or improving the plan of plant layout, certain techniques or tools are developed and are in common use today. The techniques or tools are as follows :

i) *Charts and Diagrams :* In order to achieve work simplification, production engineers make use of several charts and diagrams for summarising and analysing production process and procedures. These include :

(a) *Operation Process chart :* It subdivides the process into its separate operations and inspections. When a variety of parts and products are manufactured which follow different parts across several floor areas, an operation process chart may be necessary for the important material items or products. The flow lines on the chart indicate the sequence of all operations in the manufacturing cycle.

(b) *Flow process chart :* This chart is a graphic summary of all the activities taking place on the production floor of an existing plant. By preparing this type of a chart, it can be found out as to where operations can be eliminated, rearranged, combined, simplified or sub-divided for greater economy. This chart will also identity inflexible processes which cannot be adapted to the output of redesigned models or related outputs.

(c) *Process flow diagram :* The diagram is both supplement and substitute of process flow chart. It helps in tracing the movement of material on a floor plan or layout drawing. A diagram may be drawn to scale on the original floor plan to show the movement of work. It is a good technique to show long material hauls and backtracking of present layouts, thereby indicating how the present layout may be improved.

The flow of several standard products can be shown by coloured lines.

This diagram can be used to analyse the effectiveness of the arrangement of plant activities, the location of specific machines, and the allocation of space. It shows how a more logical arrangement and economical flow of work can be devised.

(2) *Machine data card :* This card provides full information necessary for the placement and layout of equipment. The cards are prepared separately for each machines. The information generally given on these cards include facts about the machine such as capacity of the machine, space occupied, power requirements, handling devices required and dimensions.

(3) *Templates :* Template is the drawing of a machine or tool cut out from the sheet of paper. The area occupied by a machine is shown by cutting to scale. The plant layout engineer prepares a floor plan on the basis of relevant information made available to him. Templates representing machines, tools, conveyors, furnaces, ovens, inspection stations, tanks, storages, bins, trucks etc. are then laid out on the floor plan according to the

sequence or groupings indicated on the operation process chart and the overall layout plan prepared by the engineers and helps in trying out at possible alternative arrangements. The template technique is an important technique because : (i) It eliminates unnecessary handlings, (ii) Minimised backtracking of materials, (iii) It make the mechanical handling possible, (iv) It provides a visual picture of the proposed or existing plan of layout at one place, (v) It offer flexibility to meet future changes in production requirements.

(4) *Scale models :* Though two-dimensional templates are now in extensive use in the field of layout engineering but it is not of much use to executives who cannot understand and manipulate them. One important drawback of template technique is that it leaves the volume, depth, height and clearances of machines to imagination of the reader of the drawing. These drawbacks of template technique have been removed through the development of miniature scale models of machinery and equipment cast in metal.

With scale models, it has now become possible to move

tiny figures of men and machines around in miniature factors. The miniature machines and models of material handling equipment are placed in a miniature plant and moved about like pawn on a chessboard.

(5) *Layout drawings :* Completed layouts are generally represented by drawings of the plant showing walls columns, stairways, machines and other equipment, storage areas and office areas.

The above techniques and tools are used for the planning of layout for the new plant.

Construction of Plant Building

For effective and efficient operation of the plant, design of the building is one of the main considerations. The building housing the plant should be designed in such a way that it can meet the requirements of the concern's operations and its layout. According to James Lundy, "An ideal plant building is one which is built to house the most efficient layout that can be provided for the process involved, yet which is architecturally ultra active and of such a standard shape and design as most flexible in its use and expensive units construction."

The layout may be said to be efficient if it is housed in

a building that ensures comfort and health of workers engaged on the plant with reference to heat, light, humidity, circulation of air etc. and on the other hand, it protects the plant and equipment and materials from weather.

There are several factors which are to be considered in constructing a new building for housing the plant. These are :

(i) *Adaptability* : The building structure should be adaptable fully to the needs and requirements of the plant. In the beginning, most of the enterprises carry their business in rented building which is generally not suitable to the needs and special requirements of the industries with the obvious reason that landlord constructs the building to suit average conditions of a manufacturing unit and they cannot be persuaded to make the necessary changes affecting the flexibility. As to the degree of adaptability, it may be needed that buildings are more easily adapted to fit the needs of the continuous process than to those of any other.

(ii) *Provision for additions and extensions* : In designing and constructing a new factory building, care must be taken to provide for additions and extensions which may arise to meet the necessary and peculiar needs in due course of time. There must be every possibility to add new units without disturbing the existing manufacturing system. Kimball and Kimball has rightly suggested that "an ideal building plan is one built on some 'unit' system like a sectional book case, so that additional units can be added at any time without disturbing the manufacturing system and organisation". As a general rule extension can be made most conveniently at right angles to the direction of flow of work.

(iii) Number of storeys : Another important decision while designing new plant building is to consider the number of storeys to be built, Le., whether the building should be single-storeyed or multi-storeyed. The choice between single and multi-storeys depends obviously on various factors such as nature of the product, proposed layout, value of land, the cost of construction. Before taking a decision regarding number of storeys, the management should bear in mind the comparative advantages and disadvantages of one storey and many storeys.

77